IMPRISONED
EMOTION

JOE MENDOZA

WRITERS REPUBLIC L.L.C.
515 Summit Ave. Unit R1
Union City, NJ 07087, USA

Website: *www.writersrepublic.com*
Hotline: *1-877-656-6838*
Email: *info@writersrepublic.com*

Ordering Information:
Quantity sales. Special discounts are available on quantity purchases by corporations, associations, and others. For details, contact the publisher at the address above.

Library of Congress Control Number: 2020924195
ISBN-13:   978-1-64620-818-0   [Paperback Edition]
            978-1-64620-819-7   [Digital Edition]

Rev. date: 12/04/2020

To my sons, angels in their own right. Watching over me on Earth, and now in Heaven!

You breathe a sweeter breath these days, absent of all ailment
Streets of gold caress your soles, in place of earthly pavement
A cherub's life from this day forth, you soar above the clouds
In the hearts and minds of all you knew, we couldn't be more proud
Though young in age, nevertheless, wise beyond your years
The loss of you stretched near and far, the whole world shed a tear
Courageously, you dawned a smile, though knowing we would part
Thus the legend of Super J, lives forever in our hearts!

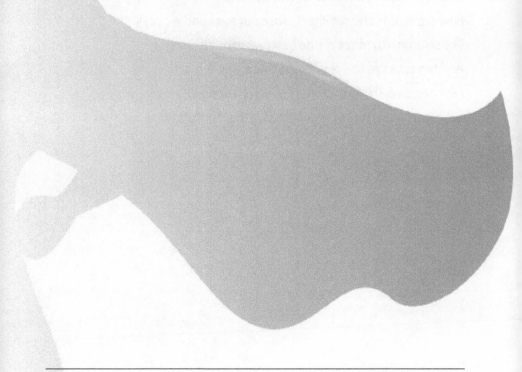

How long can a broken heart beat?

Can the pieces still feel? Will its vessels still bleed?

How long can a fragile mind think?

Can it still form a thought? Will it still be succinct?

How long can a saddened eye cry?

Will its tears all dry up? Will it one day go blind?

How long will a soul feel astray?

Will it forever stay lost? Will it still find its way?

Bereft of the answers, we turn to our faith.

Bow our heads and we kneel, close our eyes and we pray.

The strength to move on, he bestows in our hearts.

And the courage to live without those that depart.

Fear not, says the Father. You'll join us one day.

With your son there to greet you, we'll open the gates!

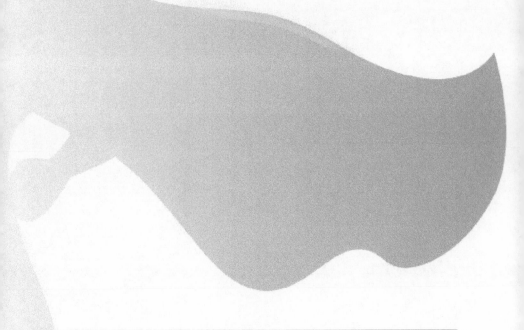

Into the light, you left the world, Heaven now the purview.

The hand of Christ now leads you forth, and darkness lies behind you.

Robbed were we, of expected time, knowing not your purpose.

By His design, you carried out, the wishes of his service.

You left the world a better place, to all whose paths you graced.

Leaving here a legacy that could never be erased.

The soundtrack of your life, though it stopped at age 11,

In turn "we'll never give you up," on Earth, as it is in heaven.

RIP, Super J! Gone but not forgotten!

Another birthday comes and goes, the world spins as it's expected.
The ails of time stand still for you, you're no longer effected.
Though here on Earth, we think we live, you're truly living life.
Our cycled days are meaningless, as we waste them biding time.
It's hard to feel we're lucky, simply cuz we still stand here.
When the pain of how we lost you, we must live with year to year.
Though counting all the days that passed, with memories of your love...
Each year we live, brings us closer to, reuniting up above!

What are visiting hours in heaven? I'd go if they exist.

For the chance to see and hear again, the angel we all miss.

Every moment since you left, is painful to get by.

And every day we look to God and ask the question "Why?"

Our hearts and minds filled with pain, that continues to consume.

A soul this world deserved to have, taken far too soon.

Lord, tell me what's your policy, tell me what must be done.

To get the chance for one last time, to visit with my son!

The blowing winds kiss your name upon my ear.

Between the raindrops, your shadow still appears.

Small mementos burning memories in my brain,

Of which the fondest, are the ones that cause most pain.

Though the fires of my soul burn a paler shade of red,

The echoes of your song resonate inside my head.

The world now sings along with you, can't seem to get enough.

We all chime in in unity, "Never gonna give you up!"

Another year has come and passed
Another turn of the hourglass
Reflecting on decision made
How lives have changed or stayed the same
Turning over all our leaves
Making goals we'll try to keep
NO matter what we've all been through
Now's our chance to start anew
Most of all, in this new year
Give thanks to God, we're all still here!

My eyes have never known sorrow, until you left their sight
My arms have never longed to hold another quite so tight
A breath had never left my lips except when I exhaled
But each day you take it from my chest when thoughts of you regale
A better fit throughout the world, you certainly won't find
Than the seamless bond that you create when you place your hand in mine
Kismet sought to cross our paths, a blessing from above
As we celebrate year after year, the day we fell in love

A muted voice to speak my mind
A broken clock to tell the time
An inkless pen to write a rhyme
Stripped of wings and forced to fly
Still I speak and find the might
To stand for what is just and right
To forge ahead and fight the flight
To walk the dark in search of light
Unwavered in my quest to find
Enlightenment inside my mind
Praise to him for every chance
To wake each day and take a stance

A father, a son, a brother, a friend
All the people I've met and the places I've been
The lives that I've touched who in turn have touched mine
Gave the best gift of all, the gift of their time
Blessed to be here, loved and alive
It's the people around me that strengthen my life
So here's to another year on this Earth
And the family and friends that give my life worth

I crack a smile just because
When thoughts of her arise
I lose myself in time and place when I gave into her eyes
As if a cure for all that ails cascaded from her lips
She breathes the life back into me each time I feel her kiss
The memory of all her curves cemented in my hands
Longing to caress her face with every given chance
Though it pains to be apart, the opposite is true
I've never felt as loved before as I do when I'm with you

A catacomb of finite sorrow
Sheaths a pessimistic morrow
Aware of the existing pit
Somehow still I seem to slip
One could paint me masochist
To see me brave it, yet persist
I trek the same familiar path
At which whose end I bear its wrath
Hoping that each time anew
I'll find a sign, a hint, a clue
Of what's ahead and what's to come
And if this journey leads to love
Lest I fail, be it all for not
Then tomorrow again I'll resume the plot

Another prospect come and gone
This game of chess, I played the pawn
Naivety would steer me wrong
Same old story, same sad song
Blind to all apparent signs
Victim to a sheltered mind
Contemplating my next path
Rebuilding in the aftermath
Seemingly a doleful sate
Reluctantly I wipe the slate
Letting hindsight navigate
Determined to fulfill the space
Left vacant by each one before
And cast away without remorse
Tomorrow's dawn with it brings
The chance for even greater things
Making sure each step resounds
I forge ahead until she's found

Our eclectic tastes and unique styles
The way we sit back, watch and smile
Few related to how we live
Less can match how much we give
A touch of this, a dash of that
Eye of newt and wing of bat
Clumsy, quirky yet profound
A witty, timid, humble clown
A myriad of social skills
Yet mute at times against our wills
A labyrinth of awkwardness
Simplistic in our happiness
We fly our flags for all to see
A salute to "Goobers" just like me

The metronomic footsteps hastened ever growing nearer
Her peripherals catch a glance of a casted shadow getting clearer
She ducked into the darkness hoping he would change his course
With frantic haste she pulled at every bolted alley door
Vaguely through the vapors of the chilly moonlit fog
Emerged a burly silhouette, panting like a dog
She threw her hands up winced away preparing for the worst
He reached for her and in her hands, he gently placed her purse
"I'm from the diner up the street, you left this in your seat"
She then relaxed letting out a sigh of great relief
"I thought that you had followed me and meant to do me harm
I see that now that's not the case, no reason for alarm"
"No worries, ma'am," he said to her, while taking off his coat
"But next time trust your instincts, bitch" and he slit her throat...

A good night's sleep, a sunny day
No chores to do, no bills to pay
Brand-new clothes and perfect hair
The smell of breakfast in the air
Commute to work, no cars in sight
Perfect timing, all green lights
Boss is sick, work half a day
Computers crash, sent home with pay
Played the lotto, scratched and won
Bought some more and won a ton
Arrived at home to surprise the wife
I called to her but no reply
I heard the voice of another man
And walked into find my neighbor Stan
Tangled in my brand-new sheets
From out one end poked four bare feet
I tiptoed out and let them be
And left a note for her to see
I hope you're happy being poor
I won a "mill," you stupid whore
Good luck to you and what's his name
I'm leaving town with his wife Jane

Life's a curveball, swift of feet
Hidden roads and nameless streets
An enigmatic questionnaire
A multi-option, dual player
To and fro and all around
Here and there and upside down
Utopiatic overdose
Tedious and comatose
Questions found to answers lost
Blood that's shed at any cost
Cataclysmic ironies
Word of mouth discrepancies
For all we learn and all we lose
Because of HIM we now can chose
Biding time, surmounting strife
'Til rebirth in the afterlife

Her painted toes, her braided hair
Her sweet perfume, her funny stares
Her quirky laugh, her lotioned hands
The way she sleeps, the way she stands
The way she sings, the way she talks
The way she trips each time she walks
The food she cooks that's sometimes burnt
The times she's gone, I wish she weren't
Her freckled face, her perfect teeth
The way she danced with two left feet
For all her faults, I couldn't see
A life without her next to me
To me she's perfect as can be
Only God knows why that she chose me

A mirrored image without a trace, of what used to be her lovely face.

Next to me now lies the place, she occupied when we embraced.

My empty hands with her she filled my lonely lips with her she sealed.

A beauty words could not describe a winning smile she couldn't hide.

I'd lose it all to have her back if nothing else this one wish grant.

I pray to thee, the Lord above, please return the one I love.

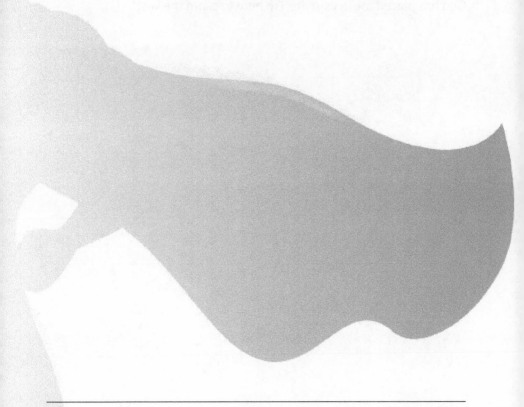

She kept her heart under lock and key and vowed she'd never love,
After so many nights spent on her knees praying he would come.
Loneliness engulfed her soul and filled her heart with ire.
Her copious tears entangled her in insurmountable mire.
A happenstance encounter changed her whole outlook on life.
She found the man she hoped one day would make this girl his wife.
He dropped to a knee and whispered, "Faith led you to me.
God has placed me in your life, I'm here to claim the key!"

An ever-present rain cloud has shadowed me my life.

Much like the cloud, torrential tears, no stranger to my eyes.

It's ominous immensity devouring all my hopes,

The courses wrought undoubtedly depravity evoked.

But through the mist and speckled dew, an aura soon appears.

A helping hand extends to me and dries away my tears.

She then leans in and says to me, "No longer the pariah.

With faith in him, he'll shelter you. Let God be your umbrella."

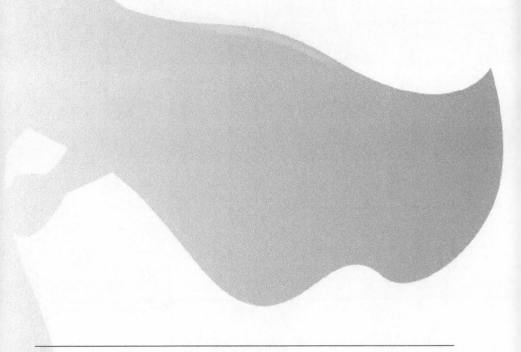

Because I've said, I think she knows
But that's not enough, you have to show
A gesture or a symbol of
What makes this girl your one true love
For the poems write she is my muse
In hopes of never her love to lose
So here's to you, my lovely rose
Now with that being said...I know she knows!

To find the hidden path that leads
to the organ from which emotion bleeds.
You'll pass through hate and happiness
to a sad and lonely emptiness.
A place where love had lived before
and patiently waits to be restored.
A missing piece, a page that's torn
like a beautiful rose with a prickly thorn.
If you've made it this far then I know
My love has found its way back home.

I know two is company and 3's a crowd
But I'd take either cuz I'm alone now.
A lonely house, a lonely bed
a hungry heart that can't be fed
My cries for help fall on deaf ears
As lonely days turn into years.
I can only hope that someday soon
I can find someone else that's lonely too.

For true loves embrace and her cheerful laughter
I'd spend this life and the one thereafter
solemnly devoted to the one who returns my "I love yous."

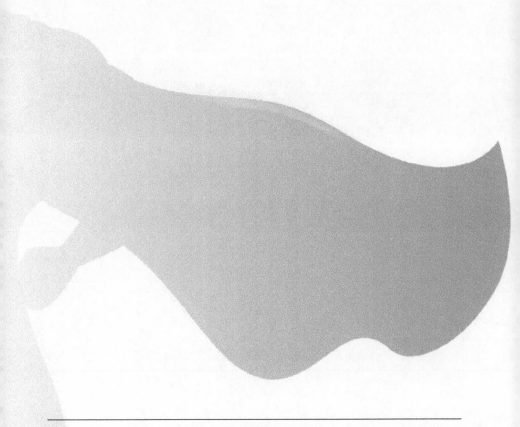

If love is beautiful and life is art
Take out a pencil and draw me a heart.
As lifeless and limp as the paper it's on
My heart is as empty as the one you have drawn.

I'd begun to scale the walls that led to a heart that lie in waiting.
Going on faith alone that once it's mine that she would my lady.
Trudging through the dying embers from the times that she'd been burned,
through the pools of wasted tears brought on by the lessons she would learn.
The kismet laced ideals of a happy ever after
lied dormant here collecting dust with the little signs of rapture.
The arduous trek would seem for most a total waste of time.
But if you could feel a love like this, you too would make the climb!

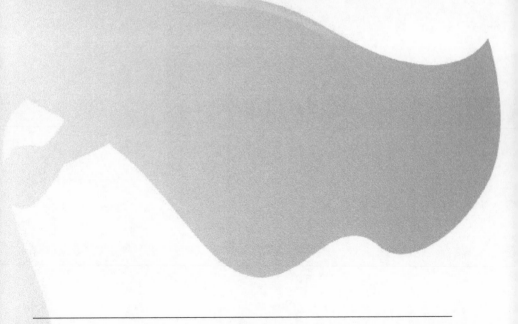

Plagiarizing smiles to hide clandestine inner thoughts
Fall in line amidst the drones as though our souls were bought
Purging every remnants of who we truly are
Conforming to society's ideally measured bar
I join the mass of mutinies who chose to break the mold
My individuality could na'er be bought or sold
Never to apologize for the person that I am
Or live my life according to a trepidatious plan
Forge your path and stay steadfast no matter where it leads
And let the inner you shine through for all the world to see

The gripping hands of solitude have cast their stones on me
They barricade each path I take and dim each light I see
I bear a crown with no recourse so heavily it weighs
Forcing me to hang my head, sedated in malaise
Each step taken seemingly with iron-weighted feet
Against the gales of hindrance, progression soon depletes
A spectacle to those who see this shadow of a man
Not knowing what I'll face each day or even if I can
Would that I could find the one to free me from this daze
To be the one I live life for until my dying days

One day here, the next day gone
Every sunset followed by its dawn
Each day comes and goes so fast
Like the sands of time through the hourglass
Cherish all the smaller things
And each memento life may bring
A random kiss, a wave good-bye
A shoulder lent for her to cry
A playful wink, a soothing hug
A warm embrace to keep her sung
Stare into each other's eyes
Wipe away each tear she cries
Be each other's better half
Be the one that makes her laugh
If you should find that someone who
Will vow to give their heart to you
Tell them that you love them so
Hold them close and don't let them go

Her cruel intentions be not lucid
Delivered from the bow of Cupid
Blinded by our heart's desires
Quickly sparks turn into fires
We see not what she turns us to
No longer us, but someone new
The convalescence we once sought
Forgotten now and all for not
Never learning from this vice
Victims of our own device
Still we stumble, trip and fall
And gladly we go through it all
Eternally in danger of
The grips of life's cruel mistress...LOVE

Unencumbered shadowed solace
Protect from what's unjust and lawless
Verdict, self-induced reclusion
Invoking fear and disillusion
Peace be found behind the cloak
Hoping ne'er you'd be provoked
Cowardly you try to hide
Behind the walls inside your mind
Ascend from darkness into light
Mustering your inner might
Forge through what may lie ahead
Ignoring all that will be said
Know that you are not alone
HE watches over from his throne
Faith be your companion too
As long as you believe in YOU!

Looking down his destined path ne'er a light is seen for miles
Despite his inner demon feuds, the sad clown wears a smile
His never faulting disposition seemingly steadfast
He shows a painted grin to all but keeps his feelings masked
Accustomed they're all for him to lighten up their moods
But who will do the same for him when sadness starts to brood
Another day thus comes and goes, he does what he's expected
All the while without surmise, his own soul he neglected
In the end what they don't see, has crippled him inside
But this accord he'll carry on, and behind the smile hide

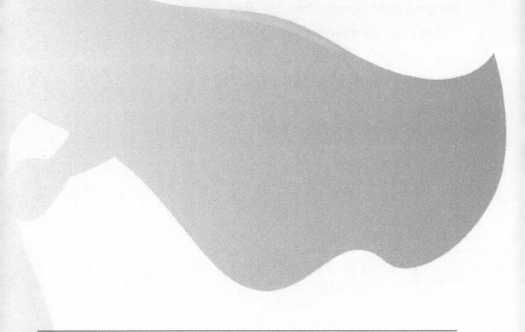

Wretched, feeble perpetration
Cause of all my trepidation
Shackled by its cruel desires
Trekking saturated mires
Routinely being led astray
Much to blame for my dismay
Strangely all for not, it be
At times, provides tranquility
Gracing both the spectrum ends
Equally it makes amends
Brings us good as well as bad
Makes us happy, makes us sad
Double-edged be this sheathed sword
But still we welcome its discord
As much as we may wish to part
We'd ne'er exist without our heart

Finding love long since discovered
Beneath a cloak of sadness, covered
Reluctantly my trust I gave
What was left, what could be saved
Bringing with each passing morrow
Hopes of ceding from my sorrow
Would that she could be the one
Thoughts of solitude undone
Like a game she played me well
Enraptured in her beauty's spell
Clumsily I fell surcease
From all that I had once believed
She left as swiftly as she came
But on my heart tattooed her name
An artifice of cruel desire
Self-induced pedantic mire
Broken hearts bring lessons learned
My love next time not easily earned

Drops of rain maraud the earth like cacophonous symphonies
As if with it we wash away our insecurities
To some the gentle *plik* and *plak* is soothing to the ear
When others hear the thunderous drench it quickly triggers fear
To me the tranquil splashes bring a lassitude effect
Enraptured in the warmth and in the comfort of my bed
I pass the storm sublimely nestled by the downpour's bliss
If only now I had someone to share this moment with

Cupid's arrow missed the mark
It hit my head and not my heart
Now instead of love I find
Imprisonment inside my mind
Reluctantly expressing thoughts
For fear of every woman's plot
Cursed to overanalyze
Untrusting of my jaded eyes
She could have walked into my life
She could have someday been my wife
Because I fell once, long ago
A new love, I may never know
Winged cherub breaks the spell
And free me from this lonely hell
Blind, but now I wish to see
So strum again your bow for me

The way I speak, the way I dress
The imperfections I confess
The things I've said, my attitude
The times I've simply been too rude
The way I laugh, the way I cry
The way I fail, the way I try
The way I hurt, the way I hate
The way each day I wipe the slate
The way I help, the way I give
This way of life I've chose to live
I endear myself to all I can
To the rest I just don't give a damn
And for all the facets you don't see
Without them I would not be me

A yeoman lover void of hope, besmirched by his first love
His breath of air, his better half, his life-sustaining drug
Jaded now, reduced to a mere semblance of a man
Writhing from his heart's desires, not knowing if he can
Feel the way he felt before for someone that's not her
Or bide his time in solitude until this life's over
A sudden change comes over him and triggers a turnstile
Brought on in passing by a woman's concupiscent smile
Seemingly rejuvenated he came to realize
To find a love anew, you need but open up your eyes

Every whisper in the dark is of my own,
every shadow is mine alone.
Every footstep heard is made by me,
every breath of air is one I breathed.
Every sun that sets alone I see,
every starlit sky, every moonlit scene.
Every stir of echoes, every word I speak,
every lonely day, every lonely week.
Every hour gone, every second passed, is just as lonely as the last.
"Everys" in my life, with them bring a daily strife.
Would that I find that one for me, so that days that I'm loved are EVERY.

Down a spiraled cobbled road, bloodied feet meet unpaved stone
Bearing gales of thunderous wind, I carry on, I must ascend
Trudging onward scaling mires, In search of that which I desire
Endless pits and jagged rock, forging my way to the top
Navigating with my heart, blindly trekking through the dark
The emanating light in sight, I summon my last bit of might
At last the pinnacle I reach, and find that which my soul doth seek
Faithfully I sought him out, and rid the devil of his clout
Salvation would now be my fate, I'm welcomed through the pearly gates
The journey is a test of life, the destination worth the strife

For every left there is a right
For every day there is a night
As every eye will covet sight
Every struggle has its plight
Life is ying, combined with yang
It ebbs it flows, again, again
For all that's good, there must be bad
An equal balance must be had
We are all but halves of wholes
In search with whom to share our souls
To fit the puzzle of our life
The missing piece we strive to find
The one to whom you stay devout
And simply can't live life without
So find who's worthy of your heart
And pray someday you'll never part

Another prospect come and gone
This game of chess, I played the pawn
Naivety would steer me wrong
Same old story, same sad song
Blind to all apparent signs
Victim to a sheltered mind
Contemplating my next path
Rebuilding in the aftermath
Seemingly a doleful state
Reluctantly I wipe the slate
Letting hindsight navigate
Determined to fulfill the space
Left vacant by each one before
And cast away without remorse
Tomorrow's dawn with it brings
The chance for even greater things
Making sure each step resounds
I forge ahead until she's found

A catacomb of finite sorrow

Sheaths a pessimistic morrow

Aware of the existing pit

Somehow still I seem to slip

One could paint me masochist

To see me brave it, yet persist

I trek the same familiar path

At which who's end I bear its wrath

Hoping that each time anew

I'll find a sign, a hint, a clue

Of what's ahead and what's to come

And if this journey leads to love

Lest I fail, be it all for not

Then tomorrow again I'll resume the plot

CPSIA information can be obtained
at www.ICGtesting.com
Printed in the USA
LVHW091935120121
675849LV00008B/890